MIGHTY IS OUR GOD

25 Songs Of Worship And Praise

Vocal • Guitar

ISBN 0-634-07378-8

HAL•LEONARD®
CORPORATION
7777 W. BLUEMOUND RD. P.O. BOX 13819 MILWAUKEE, WI 53213

Visit Hal Leonard Online at
www.halleonard.com

ABOVE ALL

Words and Music by PAUL BALOCHE
and LENNY LeBLANC

ALL THINGS ARE POSSIBLE

Words and Music by
DARLENE ZSCHECH

BE GLORIFIED

Words and Music by
BILLY FUNK

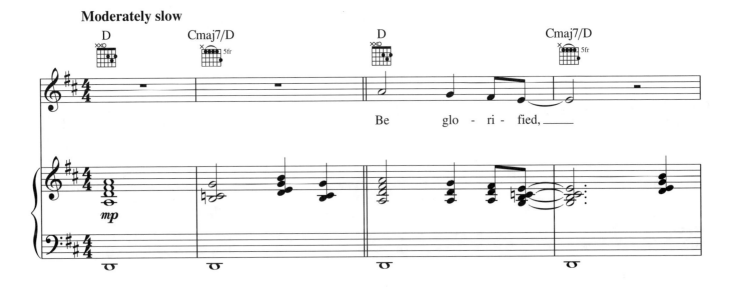

Be glo-ri-fied, ____

be glo-ri-fied. ____ Be glo-ri-fied, ____

be glo-ri-fied. ____ Be glo-ri-fied ____ in the heav-
Wor-ship You, Lord, ____ in the heav-

BREATHE

Words and Music by
MARIE BARNETT

With emotion

CELEBRATE THE LORD OF LOVE

Words and Music by PAUL BALOCHE
and ED KERR

DRAW ME CLOSE

Words and Music by
KELLY CARPENTER

FIRM FOUNDATION

Words and Music by NANCY GORDON
and JAMIE HARVILL

FOR THE LORD IS GOOD

Words and Music by LYNN DeSHAZO
and GARY SADLER

I CAN ONLY IMAGINE

Words and Music by
BART MILLARD

PRAISE ADONAI

Words and Music by
PAUL BALOCHE

I NEED YOU MORE

Words and Music by LINDELL COOLEY
and BRUCE HAYNES

Moderately slow, in 2

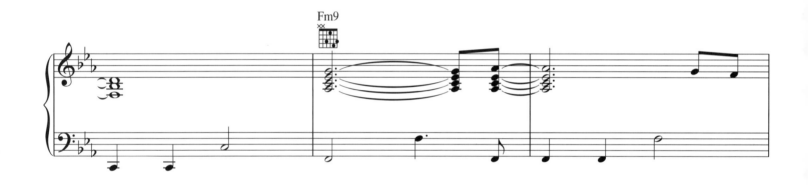

I need ___ You more, ___

I STAND IN AWE

Words and Music by
MARK ALTROGGE

I'M FOREVER GRATEFUL

Words and Music by
MARK ALTROGGE

IN THE PRESENCE

Words and Music by
MARK ALTROGGE

LET EVERYTHING THAT HAS BREATH

Words and Music by
RICHARD GOMEZ

LORD MOST HIGH

Words and Music by DON HARRIS
and GARY SADLER

MIGHTY IS OUR GOD

Words and Music by EUGENE GRECO,
GERRIT GUSTAFSON and DON MOEN

MOURNING INTO DANCING

Words and Music by
TOMMY WALKER

With rhythmic energy

He's turned my mourn - ing in - to danc - ing __ a - gain. He's

lift - ed __ my sor - row, and I can't stay si - lent. I must

66

68

ONLY BY GRACE

Words and Music by
GERRIT GUSTAFSON

OPEN THE EYES OF MY HEART

Words and Music by
PAUL BALOCHE

THE POTTER'S HAND

Words and Music by
DARLENE ZSCHECH

RISE UP AND PRAISE HIM

Words and Music by PAUL BALOCHE
and GARY SADLER

THINK ABOUT HIS LOVE

Words and Music by
WALT HARRAH

WORTHY, YOU ARE WORTHY

Words and Music by
DON MOEN

SING FOR JOY

Words and Music by
LAMONT HIEBERT